D0710304

Let's Play Hopscotch

By Sarah Hughes

Children's Press
A Division of Grolier Publishing
New York / London / Hong Kong / Sydney
Danbury, Connecticut

Photo Credits: Cover and all photos by Thaddeus Harden
Contributing Editor: Mark Beyer
Book Design: Michael DeLisio

Visit Children's Press on the Internet at:
http://publishing.grolier.com

Cataloging-in-Publication Data

Hughes, Sarah, 1964-
    Let's play hopscotch / by Sarah Hughes.
      p. cm.—(Play time)
    Includes bibliographical references and index.
    Summary: Rosa and her friends play hopscotch and
explain the steps of the game.
    ISBN 0-516-23112-X (lib. bdg.)—ISBN 0-516-23037-9 (pbk.)
    1.   Hopscotch—Juvenile literature   [1.   Hopscotch]
I.   Title   II.   Series
    2000
796.2—dc21

Contents

My name is Rosa.

I like to play **hopscotch** with my friends.

We play hopscotch in the park.

5

We draw the hopscotch lines on the ground.

We use **chalk** to draw eight **squares**.

We write eight numbers in the squares.

7

We use stones or sticks as our **markers**.

I throw my marker in square number one.

The marker has to land inside the square.

9

I hop over square number one.

I don't hop in the square with the marker.

11

I land in square number two.

I must hop on one foot to jump to each square.

13

Look at squares four and five.

Their boxes are side by side.

Mary lands on two feet for the squares that are side by side.

15

Now John is on boxes seven and eight.

These are the last boxes in the **row**.

He hops and turns around.

17

Then John hops back to the start.

He knows to hop on one foot for one square.

He knows to hop on two feet for squares that are side by side.

19

The first person to go from one to eight and back again wins.

Mary, John, and I like to play hopscotch together.

New Words

chalk (**chawk**) soft rock that can be used for drawing

hopscotch (**hop**-skoch) a game in which you jump on squares

markers (**mark**-ers) sticks or stones used to toss in hopscotch squares

row (**roh**) a line of things one after another

squares (**skwairs**) boxes with four sides

To Find Out More

Books

Hopscotch, Hangman,
Hot Potato, and Ha, Ha, Ha:
A Rulebook
of Children's Games
By Jack MacGuire
Simon & Schuster Trade

Hopscotch Around the World
By Karen Milone,
Mary D. Lankford
William Morrow
& Company

Web sites
Games Kids Play
www.gameskidsplay.net
Find dozens of kids' games with their rules at this site.

Richardson School – Best Games in a Small World
www.richardsonps.act.edu.au
This site has many new games that you can learn to play.

Index

About the Author
Sarah Hughes is from New York City and taught school for twelve years. She is now writing and editing children's books. In her free time she enjoys running and riding her bike.

Reading Consultants
Kris Flynn, Coordinator, Small School District Literacy, The San Diego County Office of Education

Shelly Forys, Certified Reading Recovery Specialist, W.J. Sahnow Elementary School, Waterloo, IL

Peggy McNamara, Professor, Bank Street College of Education, Reading and Literacy Program